Name: _____

Adress: _____

Phone: _____

Congregation: _____

MEETING TIMES

Public Talk / Wachtower Study

Day: _____ Time: _____

Our Christian Life and Ministry Meeting

Day: _____ Time: _____

Kingdom Hall Adress:

_____

ZOOM MEETING DATA

ID: _____

Code: _____ _____

BIBLE READING TRACKER

HEBREW-ARAMAIC SCRIPTURES

Genesis

1 2 3 4 5 6 7 8 9 10 11 12 13 14 15 16 17 18 19 20 21 22 23 24 25 26 27 28
○ ○

29 30 31 32 33 34 35 36 37 38 39 40 41 42 43 44 45 46 47 48 49 50
○ ○

Exodus

1 2 3 4 5 6 7 8 9 10 11 12 13 14 15 16 17 18 19 20 21 22 23 24 25 26 27 28
○ ○

29 30 31 32 33 34 35 36 37 38 39 40
○ ○ ○ ○ ○ ○ ○ ○ ○ ○ ○ ○

Leviticus

1 2 3 4 5 6 7 8 9 10 11 12 13 14 15 16 17 18 19 20 21 22 23 24 25 26 27
○ ○

Numbers

1 2 3 4 5 6 7 8 9 10 11 12 13 14 15 16 17 18 19 20 21 22 23 24 25 26 27 28
○ ○

29 30 31 32 33 34 35 36
○ ○ ○ ○ ○ ○ ○ ○

Deuteronomy

1 2 3 4 5 6 7 8 9 10 11 12 13 14 15 16 17 18 19 20 21 22 23 24 25 26 27 28
○ ○

29 30 31 32 33 34
○ ○ ○ ○ ○ ○

Joshua

1 2 3 4 5 6 7 8 9 10 11 12 13 14 15 16 17 18 19 20 21 22 23 24
○ ○

Judges

1 2 3 4 5 6 7 8 9 10 11 12 13 14 15 16 17 18 19 20 21
○ ○

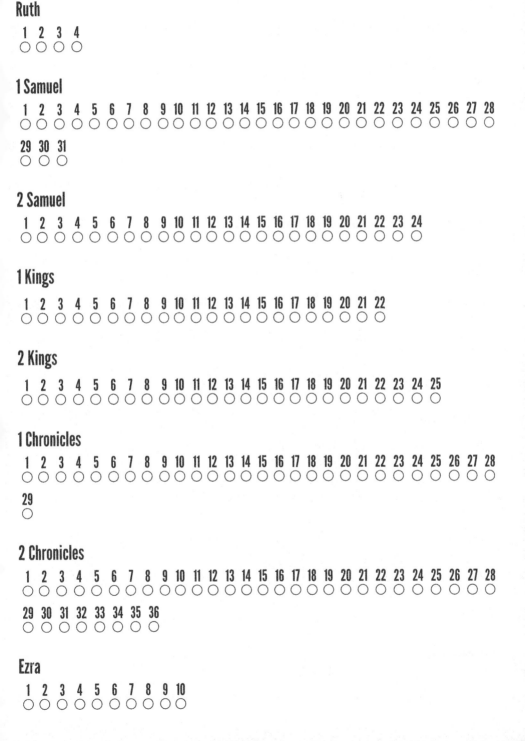

Ruth

1 2 3 4
○ ○ ○ ○

1 Samuel

1 2 3 4 5 6 7 8 9 10 11 12 13 14 15 16 17 18 19 20 21 22 23 24 25 26 27 28
○ ○

29 30 31
○ ○ ○

2 Samuel

1 2 3 4 5 6 7 8 9 10 11 12 13 14 15 16 17 18 19 20 21 22 23 24
○ ○

1 Kings

1 2 3 4 5 6 7 8 9 10 11 12 13 14 15 16 17 18 19 20 21 22
○ ○

2 Kings

1 2 3 4 5 6 7 8 9 10 11 12 13 14 15 16 17 18 19 20 21 22 23 24 25
○ ○

1 Chronicles

1 2 3 4 5 6 7 8 9 10 11 12 13 14 15 16 17 18 19 20 21 22 23 24 25 26 27 28
○ ○

29
○

2 Chronicles

1 2 3 4 5 6 7 8 9 10 11 12 13 14 15 16 17 18 19 20 21 22 23 24 25 26 27 28
○ ○

29 30 31 32 33 34 35 36
○ ○ ○ ○ ○ ○ ○ ○

Ezra

1 2 3 4 5 6 7 8 9 10
○ ○ ○ ○ ○ ○ ○ ○ ○ ○

BIBLE READING TRACKER

Nehemiah

1 2 3 4 5 6 7 8 9 10 11 12 13
○ ○ ○ ○ ○ ○ ○ ○ ○ ○ ○ ○ ○

Esther

1 2 3 4 5 6 7 8 9 10
○ ○ ○ ○ ○ ○ ○ ○ ○ ○

Job

1 2 3 4 5 6 7 8 9 10 11 12 13 14 15 16 17 18 19 20 21 22 23 24 25 26 27 28
○ ○

29 30 31 32 33 34 35 36 37 38 39 40 41 42
○ ○ ○ ○ ○ ○ ○ ○ ○ ○ ○ ○ ○ ○

Psalms

1 2 3 4 5 6 7 8 9 10 11 12 13 14 15 16 17 18 19 20 21 22 23 24 25 26 27 28
○ ○

29 30 31 32 33 34 35 36 37 38 39 40 41 42 43 44 45 46 47 48 49 50 51 52 53 54
○ ○

55 56 57 58 59 60 61 62 63 64 65 66 67 68 69 70 71 72 73 74 75 76 77 78 79 80 81
○ ○

82 83 84 85 86 87 88 89 90 91 92 93 94 95 96 97 98 99 100 101 102 103 104 105 106
○ ○

107 108 109 110 111 112 113 114 115 116 117 118 119 120 121 122 123 124 125 126 127 128 129
○ ○

130 131 132 133 134 135 136 137 138 139 140 141 142 143 144 145 146 147 148 149 150
○ ○

Proverbs

1 2 3 4 5 6 7 8 9 10 11 12 13 14 15 16 17 18 19 20 21 22 23 24 25 26 27 28
○ ○

29 30 31
○ ○ ○

Ecclesiastes

1 2 3 4 5 6 7 8 9 10 11 12
○ ○ ○ ○ ○ ○ ○ ○ ○ ○ ○ ○

~~S~~ong of Solomon

1 2 3 4 5 6 7 8
○ ○ ○ ○ ○ ○ ○ ○

~~I~~saiah

1 2 3 4 5 6 7 8 9 10 11 12 13 14 15 16 17 18 19 20 21 22 23 24 25 26 27 28
○ ○

29 30 31 32 33 34 35 36 37 38 39 40 41 42 43 44 45 46 47 48 49 50 51 52 53 54
○ ○

55 56 57 58 59 60 61 62 63 64 65 66
○ ○ ○ ○ ○ ○ ○ ○ ○ ○ ○ ○

~~J~~eremiah

1 2 3 4 5 6 7 8 9 10 11 12 13 14 15 16 17 18 19 20 21 22 23 24 25 26 27 28
○ ○

29 30 31 32 33 34 35 36 37 38 39 40 41 42 43 44 45 46 47 48 49 50 51 52
○ ○

Lamentations

1 2 3 4 5
○ ○ ○ ○ ○

Ezekiel

1 2 3 4 5 6 7 8 9 10 11 12 13 14 15 16 17 18 19 20 21 22 23 24 25 26 27 28
○ ○

29 30 31 32 33 34 35 36 37 38 39 40 41 42 43 44 45 46 47 48
○ ○ ○ ○ ○ ○ ○ ○ ○ ○ ○ ○ ○ ○ ○ ○ ○ ○ ○ ○

Daniel

1 2 3 4 5 6 7 8 9 10 11 12
○ ○ ○ ○ ○ ○ ○ ○ ○ ○ ○ ○

Hosea

1 2 3 4 5 6 7 8 9 10 11 12 13 14
○ ○ ○ ○ ○ ○ ○ ○ ○ ○ ○ ○ ○ ○

BIBLE READING TRACKER

Joel
1 2 3
○ ○ ○

Amos
1 2 3 4 5 6 7 8 9
○ ○ ○ ○ ○ ○ ○ ○ ○

Obadiah
1
○

Jonah
1 2 3 4
○ ○ ○ ○

Micah
1 2 3 4 5 6 7
○ ○ ○ ○ ○ ○ ○

Nahum
1 2 3
○ ○ ○

Habakkuk
1 2 3
○ ○ ○

Zephaniah
1 2 3
○ ○ ○

Haggai
1 2
○ ○

Zechariah
1 2 3 4 5 6 7 8 9 10 11 12 13 14
○ ○ ○ ○ ○ ○ ○ ○ ○ ○ ○ ○ ○ ○

Malachi
1 2 3 4
○ ○ ○ ○

CHRISTIAN GREEK SCRIPTURES

Matthew

1 2 3 4 5 6 7 8 9 10 11 12 13 14 15 16 17 18 19 20 21 22 23 24 25 26 27 28
○ ○

Mark

1 2 3 4 5 6 7 8 9 10 11 12 13 14 15 16
○ ○ ○ ○ ○ ○ ○ ○ ○ ○ ○ ○ ○ ○ ○ ○

Luke

1 2 3 4 5 6 7 8 9 10 11 12 13 14 15 16 17 18 19 20 21 22 23 24
○ ○

John

1 2 3 4 5 6 7 8 9 10 11 12 13 14 15 16 17 18 19 20 21
○ ○

Acts

1 2 3 4 5 6 7 8 9 10 11 12 13 14 15 16 17 18 19 20 21 22 23 24 25 26 27 28
○ ○

Romans

1 2 3 4 5 6 7 8 9 10 11 12 13 14 15 16
○ ○ ○ ○ ○ ○ ○ ○ ○ ○ ○ ○ ○ ○ ○ ○

1 Corinthians

1 2 3 4 5 6 7 8 9 10 11 12 13 14 15 16
○ ○ ○ ○ ○ ○ ○ ○ ○ ○ ○ ○ ○ ○ ○ ○

2 Corinthians

1 2 3 4 5 6 7 8 9 10 11 12 13
○ ○ ○ ○ ○ ○ ○ ○ ○ ○ ○ ○ ○

BIBLE READING TRACKER

Galatians
1 2 3 4 5 6
○ ○ ○ ○ ○ ○

Ephesians
1 2 3 4 5 6
○ ○ ○ ○ ○ ○

Philippians
1 2 3 4
○ ○ ○ ○

Colossians
1 2 3 4
○ ○ ○ ○

1 Thessalonians
1 2 3 4 5
○ ○ ○ ○ ○

2 Thessalonians
1 2 3
○ ○ ○

1 Timothy
1 2 3 4 5 6
○ ○ ○ ○ ○ ○

2 Timothy
1 2 3 4
○ ○ ○ ○

Titus
1 2 3
○ ○ ○

Philemon
1
○

Hebrews
1 2 3 4 5 6 7
○ ○ ○ ○ ○ ○ ○
8 9 10 11 12 13
○ ○ ○ ○ ○ ○

James
1 2 3 4 5
○ ○ ○ ○ ○

1 Peter
1 2 3 4 5
○ ○ ○ ○ ○

2 Peter
1 2 3
○ ○ ○

1 John
1 2 3 4 5
○ ○ ○ ○ ○

2 John
1
○

3 John
1
○

Jude
1
○

Revelation
1 2 3 4 5 6 7
○ ○ ○ ○ ○ ○ ○
8 9 10 11 12 13
○ ○ ○ ○ ○ ○
14 15 16 17 18 19 20
○ ○ ○ ○ ○ ○ ○
21 22
○ ○

PUBLIC TALK

DATE _____ **SPEAKER** _____

THEME _____

_____

_____

_____

_____

_____

_____

_____

_____

_____

_____

_____

_____

_____

_____

_____

_____

_____

_____

_____

_____

_____

_____

_____

_____

_____

_____

What are the key scriptures of this talk?

What are my goals?

OUR CHRISTIAN LIFE AND MINISTRY MEETING

📅 DATE _____   📖 BIBLE READING _____

⭐ TREASURES FROM GOD'S WORD   ☐ TALK   ☐ VIDE

_____
_____
_____
_____
_____

💎 DIGGING FOR SPIRITUAL GEMS

CHAPTER/VERSE   CHAPTER/VERSE

APPLY YOURSELF TO THE FIELD MINISTRY

☐ VIDEO ☐ INITIAL CALL ☐ RETURN VISIT ☐ BIBLE STUDY ☐ TALK

Notes

How can I apply this in my service

LIVING AS CHRISTIANS

Which qualities do I want to focus?

☐ Love ☐ Joy ☐ Peace ☐ Patience ☐ Kindness ☐ Goodness

☐ Faith ☐ Midness ☐ Self-control ☐ _____ ☐ _____

GOALS AND IMPROVEMENTS

PUBLIC TALK

THEME _____
_____
_____
_____
_____
_____
_____
_____
_____
_____
_____
_____
_____
_____
_____
_____
_____
_____
_____
_____
_____
_____
_____
_____
_____
_____
_____

What are the key scriptures of this talk?

What are my goals?

OUR CHRISTIAN LIFE AND MINISTRY MEETING

📅 DATE _____   📖 BIBLE READING _____

⭐ TREASURES FROM GOD'S WORD   ☐ TALK   ☐ VIDEO

_____

_____

_____

_____

_____

💎 DIGGING FOR SPIRITUAL GEMS

CHAPTER/VERSE   CHAPTER/VERSE

APPLY YOURSELF TO THE FIELD MINISTRY

VIDEO   □ INITIAL CALL   □ RETURN VISIT   □ BIBLE STUDY   □ TALK

Notes

How can I apply this in my service

_____

_____

_____

_____

LIVING AS CHRISTIANS

Which qualities do I want to focus?

□ Love   □ Joy   □ Peace   □ Patience   □ Kindness   □ Goodness

□ Faith   □ Midness   □ Self-control   □ _____   □ _____

_____

_____

_____

GOALS AND IMPROVEMENTS

PUBLIC TALK

📅 DATE _____ **🎤 SPEAKER** _____

THEME _____

What are the key scriptures of this talk?

What are my goals?

OUR CHRISTIAN LIFE AND MINISTRY MEETING

📅 DATE _____   📖 BIBLE READING _____

⭐ TREASURES FROM GOD'S WORD   ☐ TALK   ☐ VIDEO

_____
_____
_____
_____
_____

💎 DIGGING FOR SPIRITUAL GEMS

CHAPTER/VERSE	CHAPTER/VERSE

APPLY YOURSELF TO THE FIELD MINISTRY

☐ VIDEO   ☐ INITIAL CALL   ☐ RETURN VISIT   ☐ BIBLE STUDY   ☐ TALK

Notes

_____

_____

_____

_____

How can I apply this in my service

_____

_____

_____

_____

LIVING AS CHRISTIANS

Which qualities do I want to focus?

☐ Love   ☐ Joy   ☐ Peace   ☐ Patience   ☐ Kindness   ☐ Goodness

☐ Faith   ☐ Midness   ☐ Self-control   ☐ _____   ☐ _____

_____

_____

_____

_____

_____

GOALS AND IMPROVEMENTS

_____

_____

_____

_____

_____

PUBLIC TALK

DATE _____ **SPEAKER** _____

THEME _____

_____
_____
_____
_____
_____
_____
_____
_____
_____
_____
_____
_____
_____
_____
_____
_____
_____
_____
_____
_____
_____
_____

What are the key scriptures of this talk?

_____
_____
_____
_____

What are my goals?

_____
_____
_____
_____

OUR CHRISTIAN LIFE AND MINISTRY MEETING

📅 DATE _____   📖 BIBLE READING _____

⭐ TREASURES FROM GOD'S WORD   ☐ TALK   ☐ VIDE

_____

_____

_____

_____

_____

💎 DIGGING FOR SPIRITUAL GEMS

CHAPTER/VERSE   **CHAPTER/VERSE**

APPLY YOURSELF TO THE FIELD MINISTRY

☐ VIDEO   ☐ INITIAL CALL   ☐ RETURN VISIT   ☐ BIBLE STUDY   ☐ TALK

Notes

How can I apply this in my service

LIVING AS CHRISTIANS

Which qualities do I want to focus?

☐ Love   ☐ Joy   ☐ Peace   ☐ Patience   ☐ Kindness   ☐ Goodness

☐ Faith   ☐ Midness   ☐ Self-control   ☐ _____   ☐ _____

GOALS AND IMPROVEMENTS

PUBLIC TALK

DATE _____ **SPEAKER** _____

THEME _____

_____
_____
_____
_____
_____
_____
_____
_____
_____
_____
_____
_____
_____
_____
_____
_____
_____
_____
_____
_____
_____
_____
_____

What are the key scriptures of this talk?

What are my goals?

OUR CHRISTIAN LIFE AND MINISTRY MEETING

📅 DATE _____   📖 BIBLE READING _____

⭐ TREASURES FROM GOD'S WORD   ☐ TALK   ☐ VIDEO

_____
_____
_____
_____
_____

💎 DIGGING FOR SPIRITUAL GEMS

CHAPTER/VERSE   CHAPTER/VERSE

APPLY YOURSELF TO THE FIELD MINISTRY

VIDEO   □ INITIAL CALL   □ RETURN VISIT   □ BIBLE STUDY   □ TALK

Notes

How can I apply this in my service

LIVING AS CHRISTIANS

Which qualities do I want to focus?

□ Love   □ Joy   □ Peace   □ Patience   □ Kindness   □ Goodness

□ Faith   □ Midness   □ Self-control   □ _____   □ _____

GOALS AND IMPROVEMENTS

PUBLIC TALK

DATE _____   **SPEAKER** _____

THEME _____

_____

_____

_____

_____

_____

_____

_____

_____

_____

_____

_____

_____

_____

_____

_____

_____

_____

_____

_____

_____

_____

_____

_____

_____

_____

_____

_____

_____

_____

_____

What are the key scriptures of this talk?

What are my goals?

OUR CHRISTIAN LIFE AND MINISTRY MEETING

📅 DATE _____   📖 BIBLE READING _____

⭐ TREASURES FROM GOD'S WORD   ☐ TALK   ☐ VIDEO

_____
_____
_____
_____
_____

💎 DIGGING FOR SPIRITUAL GEMS

CHAPTER/VERSE

_____
_____
_____
_____
_____
_____
_____
_____
_____
_____
_____
_____
_____

CHAPTER/VERSE

_____
_____
_____
_____
_____
_____
_____
_____
_____
_____
_____
_____
_____

APPLY YOURSELF TO THE FIELD MINISTRY

□ VIDEO □ INITIAL CALL □ RETURN VISIT □ BIBLE STUDY □ TALK

Notes

How can I apply this in my service

LIVING AS CHRISTIANS

Which qualities do I want to focus?

□ Love □ Joy □ Peace □ Patience □ Kindness □ Goodness

□ Faith □ Midness □ Self-control □ _____ □ _____

GOALS AND IMPROVEMENTS

PUBLIC TALK

DATE _____   **SPEAKER** _____

THEME _____

What are the key scriptures of this talk?

What are my goals?

OUR CHRISTIAN LIFE AND MINISTRY MEETING

📅 DATE _____   📖 BIBLE READING _____

⭐ TREASURES FROM GOD'S WORD

☐ TALK   ☐ VIDE

_____

_____

_____

_____

_____

💎 DIGGING FOR SPIRITUAL GEMS

CHAPTER/VERSE

CHAPTER/VERSE

APPLY YOURSELF TO THE FIELD MINISTRY

☐ VIDEO   ☐ INITIAL CALL   ☐ RETURN VISIT   ☐ BIBLE STUDY   ☐ TALK

Notes

How can I apply this in my service

LIVING AS CHRISTIANS

Which qualities do I want to focus?

☐ Love   ☐ Joy   ☐ Peace   ☐ Patience   ☐ Kindness   ☐ Goodness

☐ Faith   ☐ Midness   ☐ Self-control   ☐ _____   ☐ _____

GOALS AND IMPROVEMENTS

PUBLIC TALK

DATE _____   **SPEAKER** _____

THEME _____

_____
_____
_____
_____
_____
_____
_____
_____
_____
_____
_____
_____
_____
_____
_____
_____
_____
_____
_____
_____
_____
_____
_____
_____
_____

_____
_____
_____
_____
_____
_____
_____
_____
_____
_____
_____
_____
_____
_____
_____
_____
_____
_____
_____
_____
_____

What are the key scriptures of this talk?

_____
_____
_____
_____

What are my goals?

_____
_____
_____
_____

OUR CHRISTIAN LIFE AND MINISTRY MEETING

📅 DATE _____   📖 BIBLE READING _____

⭐ TREASURES FROM GOD'S WORD   ☐ TALK   ☐ VIDEO

_____
_____
_____
_____
_____

💎 DIGGING FOR SPIRITUAL GEMS

CHAPTER/VERSE   CHAPTER/VERSE

APPLY YOURSELF TO THE FIELD MINISTRY

VIDEO   ☐ INITIAL CALL   ☐ RETURN VISIT   ☐ BIBLE STUDY   ☐ TALK

Notes

How can I apply this in my service

_____   _____

_____   _____

_____   _____

_____   _____

LIVING AS CHRISTIANS

Which qualities do I want to focus?

☐ Love   ☐ Joy   ☐ Peace   ☐ Patience   ☐ Kindness   ☐ Goodness

☐ Faith   ☐ Midness   ☐ Self-control   ☐ _____   ☐ _____

_____

_____

_____

_____

_____   **GOALS AND IMPROVEMENTS**

_____   _____

_____   _____

_____   _____

_____   _____

_____   _____

PUBLIC TALK

DATE _____ **SPEAKER** _____

THEME _____

What are the key scriptures of this talk?

What are my goals?

OUR CHRISTIAN LIFE AND MINISTRY MEETING

📅 DATE _____   📖 BIBLE READING _____

⭐ TREASURES FROM GOD'S WORD
☐ TALK   ☐ VIDEO

_____

_____

_____

_____

_____

💎 DIGGING FOR SPIRITUAL GEMS

CHAPTER/VERSE

CHAPTER/VERSE

APPLY YOURSELF TO THE FIELD MINISTRY

☐ VIDEO   ☐ INITIAL CALL   ☐ RETURN VISIT   ☐ BIBLE STUDY   ☐ TALK

Notes

How can I apply this in my service

LIVING AS CHRISTIANS

Which qualities do I want to focus?

☐ Love   ☐ Joy   ☐ Peace   ☐ Patience   ☐ Kindness   ☐ Goodness

☐ Faith   ☐ Midness   ☐ Self-control   ☐ _____   ☐ _____

GOALS AND IMPROVEMENTS

PUBLIC TALK

DATE _____   **SPEAKER** _____

THEME _____

_____

_____

_____

_____

_____

_____

_____

_____

_____

_____

_____

_____

_____

_____

_____

_____

_____

_____

_____

_____

_____

_____

_____

What are the key scriptures of this talk?

What are my goals?

OUR CHRISTIAN LIFE AND MINISTRY MEETING

📅 DATE _____   📖 BIBLE READING _____

TREASURES FROM GOD'S WORD

☐ TALK   ☐ VIDE

_____
_____
_____
_____
_____

DIGGING FOR SPIRITUAL GEMS

CHAPTER/VERSE

CHAPTER/VERSE

APPLY YOURSELF TO THE FIELD MINISTRY

☐ VIDEO　　　☐ INITIAL CALL　　　☐ RETURN VISIT　　　☐ BIBLE STUDY　　　☐ TALK

Notes

How can I apply this in my service

LIVING AS CHRISTIANS

Which qualities do I want to focus?

☐ Love　　☐ Joy　　☐ Peace　　☐ Patience　　☐ Kindness　　☐ Goodness

☐ Faith　　☐ Midness　　☐ Self-control　　☐ _____　　☐ _____

GOALS AND IMPROVEMENTS

PUBLIC TALK

DATE _____   **SPEAKER** _____

THEME _____

_____

_____

_____

_____

_____

_____

_____

_____

_____

_____

_____

_____

_____

_____

_____

_____

_____

_____

_____

_____

_____

_____

_____

_____

_____

_____

_____

_____
_____
_____
_____
_____
_____
_____
_____
_____
_____
_____
_____
_____
_____
_____
_____
_____
_____
_____
_____
_____

What are the key scriptures of this talk?

_____
_____
_____
_____
_____

What are my goals?

_____
_____
_____
_____

OUR CHRISTIAN LIFE AND MINISTRY MEETING

📅 DATE _____   📖 BIBLE READING _____

✦ TREASURES FROM GOD'S WORD

□ TALK   □ VIDEO

_____
_____
_____
_____

◇ DIGGING FOR SPIRITUAL GEMS

CHAPTER/VERSE	CHAPTER/VERSE

APPLY YOURSELF TO THE FIELD MINISTRY

VIDEO   □ INITIAL CALL   □ RETURN VISIT   □ BIBLE STUDY   □ TALK

Notes

How can I apply this in my service

LIVING AS CHRISTIANS

Which qualities do I want to focus?

□ Love   □ Joy   □ Peace   □ Patience   □ Kindness   □ Goodness

□ Faith   □ Midness   □ Self-control   □ _____   □ _____

GOALS AND IMPROVEMENTS

PUBLIC TALK

📅 **DATE** _____   🎤 **SPEAKER** _____

THEME _____

_____

_____

_____

_____

_____

_____

_____

_____

_____

_____

_____

_____

_____

_____

_____

_____

_____

_____

_____

_____

_____

_____

_____

_____

_____

_____

What are the key scriptures of this talk?

What are my goals?

OUR CHRISTIAN LIFE AND MINISTRY MEETING

📅 DATE _____   📖 BIBLE READING _____

⭐ TREASURES FROM GOD'S WORD   ☐ TALK   ☐ VIDEO

_____
_____
_____
_____
_____

💎 DIGGING FOR SPIRITUAL GEMS

CHAPTER/VERSE   **CHAPTER/VERSE**

APPLY YOURSELF TO THE FIELD MINISTRY

☐ VIDEO   ☐ INITIAL CALL   ☐ RETURN VISIT   ☐ BIBLE STUDY   ☐ TALK

Notes

How can I apply this in my service

LIVING AS CHRISTIANS

Which qualities do I want to focus?

☐ Love   ☐ Joy   ☐ Peace   ☐ Patience   ☐ Kindness   ☐ Goodness

☐ Faith   ☐ Midness   ☐ Self-control   ☐ _____   ☐ _____

GOALS AND IMPROVEMENTS

PUBLIC TALK

📅 DATE _____   🎤 SPEAKER _____

THEME _____

_____

_____

_____

_____

_____

_____

_____

_____

_____

_____

_____

_____

_____

_____

_____

_____

_____

_____

_____

_____

_____

_____

_____

What are the key scriptures of this talk?

What are my goals?

OUR CHRISTIAN LIFE AND MINISTRY MEETING

📅 DATE _____   📖 BIBLE READING _____

⭐ TREASURES FROM GOD'S WORD   ☐ TALK   ☐ VIDE

_____
_____
_____
_____
_____

💎 DIGGING FOR SPIRITUAL GEMS

CHAPTER/VERSE   CHAPTER/VERSE

APPLY YOURSELF TO THE FIELD MINISTRY

☐ VIDEO   ☐ INITIAL CALL   ☐ RETURN VISIT   ☐ BIBLE STUDY   ☐ TALK

Notes

How can I apply this in my service

LIVING AS CHRISTIANS

Which qualities do I want to focus?

☐ Love   ☐ Joy   ☐ Peace   ☐ Patience   ☐ Kindness   ☐ Goodness

☐ Faith   ☐ Midness   ☐ Self-control   ☐ _____   ☐ _____

GOALS AND IMPROVEMENTS

PUBLIC TALK

📅 DATE _____   🎤 SPEAKER _____

THEME _____

_____

_____

_____

_____

_____

_____

_____

_____

_____

_____

_____

_____

_____

_____

_____

_____

_____

_____

_____

_____

_____

_____

_____

_____
_____
_____
_____
_____
_____
_____
_____
_____
_____
_____
_____
_____
_____
_____
_____
_____
_____
_____
_____
_____

What are the key scriptures of this talk?

_____

_____

_____

_____

_____

What are my goals?

_____

_____

_____

_____

OUR CHRISTIAN LIFE AND MINISTRY MEETING

📆 DATE _____   📖 BIBLE READING _____

⭐ TREASURES FROM GOD'S WORD

☐ TALK   ☐ VIDEO

_____
_____
_____
_____
_____

💎 DIGGING FOR SPIRITUAL GEMS

CHAPTER/VERSE

CHAPTER/VERSE

APPLY YOURSELF TO THE FIELD MINISTRY

VIDEO   □ INITIAL CALL   □ RETURN VISIT   □ BIBLE STUDY   □ TALK

Notes

How can I apply this in my service

LIVING AS CHRISTIANS

Which qualities do I want to focus?

□ Love   □ Joy   □ Peace   □ Patience   □ Kindness   □ Goodness

□ Faith   □ Midness   □ Self-control   □ _____   □ _____

GOALS AND IMPROVEMENTS

PUBLIC TALK

📅 DATE _____   🎤 SPEAKER _____

THEME _____

_____
_____
_____
_____
_____
_____
_____
_____
_____
_____
_____
_____
_____
_____
_____
_____
_____
_____
_____
_____
_____
_____
_____
_____
_____
_____
_____
_____
_____
_____

What are the key scriptures of this talk?

What are my goals?

OUR CHRISTIAN LIFE AND MINISTRY MEETING

📅 DATE _____   📖 BIBLE READING _____

✨ TREASURES FROM GOD'S WORD   ☐ TALK   ☐ VIDEO

_____
_____
_____
_____
_____

💎 DIGGING FOR SPIRITUAL GEMS

CHAPTER/VERSE

_____
_____
_____
_____
_____
_____
_____
_____
_____
_____
_____
_____

CHAPTER/VERSE

_____
_____
_____
_____
_____
_____
_____
_____
_____
_____
_____

APPLY YOURSELF TO THE FIELD MINISTRY

□ VIDEO   □ INITIAL CALL   □ RETURN VISIT   □ BIBLE STUDY   □ TALK

Notes

How can I apply this in my service

LIVING AS CHRISTIANS

Which qualities do I want to focus?

□ Love   □ Joy   □ Peace   □ Patience   □ Kindness   □ Goodness

□ Faith   □ Midness   □ Self-control   □ _____   □ _____

GOALS AND IMPROVEMENTS

PUBLIC TALK

📅 **DATE** _____   🎤 **SPEAKER** _____

THEME _____

_____

_____

_____

_____

_____

_____

_____

_____

_____

_____

_____

_____

_____

_____

_____

_____

_____

_____

_____

_____

_____

_____

_____

_____

What are the key scriptures of this talk?

What are my goals?

OUR CHRISTIAN LIFE AND MINISTRY MEETING

📅 DATE _____   📖 BIBLE READING _____

⭐ TREASURES FROM GOD'S WORD   ☐ TALK   ☐ VIDE

_____
_____
_____
_____
_____

💎 DIGGING FOR SPIRITUAL GEMS

CHAPTER/VERSE   **CHAPTER/VERSE**

APPLY YOURSELF TO THE FIELD MINISTRY

☐ VIDEO   ☐ INITIAL CALL   ☐ RETURN VISIT   ☐ BIBLE STUDY   ☐ TALK

Notes

How can I apply this in my service

LIVING AS CHRISTIANS

Which qualities do I want to focus?

☐ Love   ☐ Joy   ☐ Peace   ☐ Patience   ☐ Kindness   ☐ Goodness

☐ Faith   ☐ Midness   ☐ Self-control   ☐ _____   ☐ _____

GOALS AND IMPROVEMENTS

PUBLIC TALK

DATE _____ **SPEAKER** _____

THEME _____

_____
_____
_____
_____
_____
_____
_____
_____
_____
_____
_____
_____
_____
_____
_____
_____
_____
_____
_____
_____
_____
_____
_____
_____
_____
_____
_____
_____
_____
_____

What are the key scriptures of this talk?

What are my goals?

OUR CHRISTIAN LIFE AND MINISTRY MEETING

📅 DATE _____   📖 BIBLE READING _____

⭐ TREASURES FROM GOD'S WORD

☐ TALK   ☐ VIDEO

_____
_____
_____
_____

💎 DIGGING FOR SPIRITUAL GEMS

CHAPTER/VERSE

CHAPTER/VERSE

APPLY YOURSELF TO THE FIELD MINISTRY

☐ VIDEO   ☐ INITIAL CALL   ☐ RETURN VISIT   ☐ BIBLE STUDY   ☐ TALK

Notes

How can I apply this in my service

LIVING AS CHRISTIANS

Which qualities do I want to focus?

☐ Love   ☐ Joy   ☐ Peace   ☐ Patience   ☐ Kindness   ☐ Goodness

☐ Faith   ☐ Midness   ☐ Self-control   ☐ _____   ☐ _____

GOALS AND IMPROVEMENTS

PUBLIC TALK

THEME _____

_____

_____

_____

_____

_____

_____

_____

_____

_____

_____

_____

_____

_____

_____

_____

_____

_____

_____

_____

_____

_____

_____

_____

_____

_____

_____

_____

_____

What are the key scriptures of this talk?

What are my goals?

OUR CHRISTIAN LIFE AND MINISTRY MEETING

📅 DATE _____   📖 BIBLE READING _____

⭐ TREASURES FROM GOD'S WORD   ☐ TALK   ☐ VIDEO

_____
_____
_____
_____
_____

💎 DIGGING FOR SPIRITUAL GEMS

CHAPTER/VERSE   CHAPTER/VERSE

APPLY YOURSELF TO THE FIELD MINISTRY

□ VIDEO □ INITIAL CALL □ RETURN VISIT □ BIBLE STUDY □ TALK

Notes

_____

_____

_____

_____

How can I apply this in my service

_____

_____

_____

_____

LIVING AS CHRISTIANS

Which qualities do I want to focus?

□ Love □ Joy □ Peace □ Patience □ Kindness □ Goodness

□ Faith □ Midness □ Self-control □ _____ □ _____

_____

_____

_____

_____

_____

_____

_____

_____

_____

GOALS AND IMPROVEMENTS

_____

_____

_____

_____

_____

_____

PUBLIC TALK

DATE _____ **SPEAKER** _____

THEME _____

_____
_____
_____
_____
_____
_____
_____
_____
_____
_____
_____
_____
_____
_____
_____
_____
_____
_____
_____
_____
_____
_____
_____
_____
_____

What are the key scriptures of this talk?

What are my goals?

OUR CHRISTIAN LIFE AND MINISTRY MEETING

📅 DATE _____ 📖 BIBLE READING _____

TREASURES FROM GOD'S WORD
☐ TALK   ☐ VIDE

_____
_____
_____
_____
_____

💎 DIGGING FOR SPIRITUAL GEMS

CHAPTER/VERSE   CHAPTER/VERSE

APPLY YOURSELF TO THE FIELD MINISTRY

☐ VIDEO ☐ INITIAL CALL ☐ RETURN VISIT ☐ BIBLE STUDY ☐ TALK

Notes

How can I apply this in my service

LIVING AS CHRISTIANS

Which qualities do I want to focus?

☐ Love ☐ Joy ☐ Peace ☐ Patience ☐ Kindness ☐ Goodness

☐ Faith ☐ Midness ☐ Self-control ☐ _____ ☐ _____

GOALS AND IMPROVEMENTS

PUBLIC TALK

📅 **DATE** _____ 🎤 **SPEAKER** _____

THEME _____

_____
_____
_____
_____
_____
_____
_____
_____
_____
_____
_____
_____
_____
_____
_____
_____
_____
_____
_____
_____
_____
_____
_____
_____
_____
_____
_____
_____

_____

_____

_____

_____

_____

_____

_____

_____

_____

_____

_____

_____

_____

_____

_____

_____

_____

_____

_____

_____

_____

What are the key scriptures of this talk?

_____

_____

_____

_____

What are my goals?

_____

_____

_____

_____

OUR CHRISTIAN LIFE AND MINISTRY MEETING

📅 **DATE** _____   📖 **BIBLE READING** _____

⭐ TREASURES FROM GOD'S WORD   ☐ TALK   ☐ VIDEO

_____

_____

_____

_____

_____

💎 DIGGING FOR SPIRITUAL GEMS

CHAPTER/VERSE   **CHAPTER/VERSE**

APPLY YOURSELF TO THE FIELD MINISTRY

☐ VIDEO   ☐ INITIAL CALL   ☐ RETURN VISIT   ☐ BIBLE STUDY   ☐ TALK

Notes

How can I apply this in my service

LIVING AS CHRISTIANS

Which qualities do I want to focus?

☐ Love   ☐ Joy   ☐ Peace   ☐ Patience   ☐ Kindness   ☐ Goodness

☐ Faith   ☐ Midness   ☐ Self-control   ☐ _____   ☐ _____

GOALS AND IMPROVEMENTS

PUBLIC TALK

DATE _____ **SPEAKER** _____

THEME _____

_____
_____
_____
_____
_____
_____
_____
_____
_____
_____
_____
_____
_____
_____
_____
_____
_____
_____
_____
_____
_____
_____
_____
_____
_____
_____
_____

OUR CHRISTIAN LIFE AND MINISTRY MEETING

📅 DATE _____   📖 BIBLE READING _____

⭐ TREASURES FROM GOD'S WORD   ☐ TALK   ☐ VIDEO

_____

_____

_____

_____

_____

💎 DIGGING FOR SPIRITUAL GEMS

CHAPTER/VERSE   CHAPTER/VERSE

APPLY YOURSELF TO THE FIELD MINISTRY

☐ VIDEO ☐ INITIAL CALL ☐ RETURN VISIT ☐ BIBLE STUDY ☐ TALK

Notes

How can I apply this in my service

LIVING AS CHRISTIANS

Which qualities do I want to focus?

☐ Love ☐ Joy ☐ Peace ☐ Patience ☐ Kindness ☐ Goodness

☐ Faith ☐ Midness ☐ Self-control ☐ _____ ☐ _____

GOALS AND IMPROVEMENTS

PUBLIC TALK

DATE _____   **SPEAKER** _____

THEME _____

_____
_____
_____
_____
_____
_____
_____
_____
_____
_____
_____
_____
_____
_____
_____
_____
_____
_____
_____
_____
_____
_____
_____
_____
_____
_____
_____

What are the key scriptures of this talk?

What are my goals?

OUR CHRISTIAN LIFE AND MINISTRY MEETING

📅 DATE _____ 📖 BIBLE READING _____

⭐ TREASURES FROM GOD'S WORD

☐ TALK   ☐ VIDEO

_____
_____
_____
_____
_____

💎 DIGGING FOR SPIRITUAL GEMS

CHAPTER/VERSE	CHAPTER/VERSE

APPLY YOURSELF TO THE FIELD MINISTRY

□ VIDEO □ INITIAL CALL □ RETURN VISIT □ BIBLE STUDY □ TALK

Notes

How can I apply this in my service

LIVING AS CHRISTIANS

Which qualities do I want to focus?

□ Love □ Joy □ Peace □ Patience □ Kindness □ Goodness

□ Faith □ Midness □ Self-control □ _____ □ _____

GOALS AND IMPROVEMENTS

Made in the USA
Las Vegas, NV
08 January 2024

84094059R00056